CONSPIRACY
TO ASSASSINATE

President John F. Kennedy,
Dr. Martin Luther King Jr.
and Senator Robert F. Kennedy.

JOHN PATRICK ROACH JR.

CONSPIRACY
TO ASSASSINATE

President John F. Kennedy,
Dr. Martin Luther King Jr.
and Senator Robert F. Kennedy.

authorHOUSE®

AuthorHouse™ LLC
1663 Liberty Drive
Bloomington, IN 47403
www.authorhouse.com
Phone: 1-800-839-8640

Published by AuthorHouse   07/11/2013

ISBN: 978-1-4817-7448-2 (sc)
ISBN: 978-1-4817-7446-8 (hc)
ISBN: 978-1-4817-7447-5 (e)

Library of Congress Control Number: 2013912257

EDITOR: Sherri Lee Books; Assisting Editor, Grace De' Palma

FRONT COVER: The Eternal Flame. Marking the gravesite of President John F. Kennedy and his wife, Jacqueline. Located in Washington National Cemetery, Alexandria, VA.

DEDICATION

To those with Inquiring Minds.

Works of *John P. Roach Jr.*

Historical Novels

Mt. Soledad Love Story (Aristotle and Thomas Aquinas.)
CALIFORNIA-The First 100 Years (Padre Serra to the Golden Spike.)
Conspiracy to Assassinate President John F. Kennedy, M.L.K and R.F.K.

Biographical Novels

The Fourteenth State (Ethan Allen.)
Triumph of the Swan (Opera Composer Richard Wagner and King
    Ludwig II of Bavaria.)
Absinthe (Edgar Degas, Realist Artist and a Leader in the Impressionist
    Revolution.)
The Mighty Kutchka (Nikolai Rimsky-Korsakov & The Russian Five.)
Essence of an Idealist (Autobiography of a Common Man.)

Inspirational Books

Serial Monogamy (A quest for Success, Happiness and Love.)
Around the World in a Wheelchair (A motivational book for the disabled.)
Thanks for the Memories Cookbook (Deborah J. Johnson and Friends.)

Travel

Experience America's Finest City on the San Diego Trolley
Outrageous! (A Second Round the World Cruise.)

Science

Inquiring Minds (Teens challenge education system.)
The Ascent of Man (The many alternatives to Darwin's Decent of Man.)

WEBSITE

www.JPRoach.org

CONSPIRACY to ASSASSINATE

President John F. Kennedy,

Dr. Martin Luther King Jr.,

And

Senator Robert F. Kennedy.

By

JOHN PATRICK ROACH JR.

President John F. Kennedy
White House Photo

Contents

ABSTRACT

CONSPIRACY TO ASSASSINATE PRESIDENT JOHN F. KENNEDY

This book is about grasping power and once achieving it, using that power to assassinate all challengers to the power gained.

The Warren Commission Report concluded that Lee Harvey Oswald acted alone and was not part of a conspiracy, and went on to say that there is no evidence of a conspiracy. This report pacified the American public for the last 50 years.

Logic and Reason dictates otherwise. Each of us has the ability to use our own logic to determine who had the most to gain from the President John F. Kennedy assassination. However it seems unreasonable that he could do it alone and get away with it. So it doesn't pass the reason test.

Therefore, logic again comes into the equation that would require a co-conspirator capable of providing a complete cover-up, so the conspirators will never be caught.

The co-conspirators need only patsies to take the blame with promises of a fee or fame or whatever satisfies their weakness.

With the Kennedy assassination completed and blamed on Lee Harvey Oswald who is murdered before he can utter more that "I'm just a patsy," the American population seems satisfied that he paid for his crime, while the conspirators remain free.

Using the same procedure of patsies to take the rap, the conspirators assassinate Martin Luther King Jr. and Senator Robert Kennedy, a leading Democratic Candidate for President in 1968, and got away with it.

Your use of logic and reason may lead you to the same conclusion that a conspiracy of the highest magnitude took the lives of these three idealists.

INTRODUCTION

I was 26 years old when they shot our President. My car pool friend, Fred Kane, who favored Nixon in the upcoming 1960 election entered my office and said "they shot Kennedy, they shot the President!"! We both immediately went to a TV and found President Kennedy had been shot and will be taken to Parkland Hospital in Dallas.

No word yet on his condition until they finally said, "The President is dead." Fred and I both cried. After all I am 26 and loved the Camelot Kennedy created. All those idealistic dreams are now smashed.

I remained emotional over Kennedy's death for a long time. Look Magazine, 21 months later, did a special edition on the Kennedys'. In Look magazine is the photographic painting of President Kennedy that moved me so much . . .

For my first oil painting, I copied the Look Magazine painting, framed it and hung it in my study. That painting served as a reminder to me, to use my philosophical background of logic and reason in questioning the conclusions of the Warren Commission report that President Johnson had ordered upon taking office.

The 888 page Warren Commission Report presented to President Johnson 10 months later, concluded that the Kennedy assassination is the work of a single assassin and <u>not a conspiracy.</u>

I studied the great detail of the report and would agree with the Warren Commission Report conclusion that most likely Lee Harvey Oswald shot our President. Their conclusion that there was no conspiracy was like commissioning the fox to a report on the missing chickens in the hen house. Logic and reason lead me to believe there is still an unsolved conspiracy.

Thus, the title of this book.

Now 50 years later, so many wonderful authors have gathered facts and written their opinions of that time and place that once was Camelot. My intent is not to get into the life of John F. Kennedy and others around him, as so many biographers have recorded their lives so well.

Rather I intend to garner from their works that which supports the idiosyncrasies of various personalities that President Kennedy encountered. This, then, will hopefully find that link to determine and expose the masterminds of the conspiracy to assassinate President John F. Kennedy.

As I look deep into these encounters, I discover patterns that support a top down conspiracy from the very highest levels of government to assassinate not only our President, John F. Kennedy, and Senator Robert F. Kennedy, the leading Democratic Candidate for President in 1964, but the famed Civil Rights Leader, Dr. Martin Luther King Jr.—All of which took direction from the same masterminds of conspiracy.

I hope to bring the reader along the same path of logic and reason.

John Patrick Roach Jr.

Photo of the author at age 26 with his first oil painting

CHAPTER I

ASSASSINATIONS OF SIGNIFICANT WORLD LEADERS

Assassination is a word used to typically mean the targeted Killing of a public figure.

Conspiracy usually involves more than one individual who keep secret their plans.

Envy, Jealously, Covetousness, and especially Power; has prompted conspiracy so often in the past that when coupled with an assassination becomes very difficult to determine the originator.

Some examples of individual assassins and conspiracy assassinations follow:

Zechariah, King of Israel 800 BC
      Killed by Shallum who succeeded Zechariah.

Shallum, King of Israel 772 BC
      Killed by Menahem, a General who succeeded Shallum

Pakahiah, King of Israel 737 BC
      Killed by Pekah a commander who succeeded Pakahiah

Pekah, King of Israel 732 BC
> Killed by Hoshea who succeeded Pekah

Xerxes I King of Persia, 465 BC
> Killed by Artabanus The Commander of the Royal Bodyguard

Philip of Macedonia, 336 BC
> Killed by trusted friends that remains unsolved as a possible conspiracy involving his wife Olympia's desiring to have her son Alexander on the throne or perhaps even Alexander himself.

Julius Caesar, 44BC
> Thought to be gaining too much power, Caesar was killed by a conspiracy of Senators seeking over-throw and change of government from the Republic of Rome to the Roman Empire.

Arch Duke Ferdinand and his wife Sophie
> Heir to the throne of the Austria-Hungarian Empire killed by a Serbian causing alliances to both sides by many countries preceding World War I.

Grigori Rasputin, 1916
> Thought to have too much influence over Alexandra, wife of Czar Nicholas II, Rasputin was poisoned, shot three times and beaten at dinner at Yusapov Palace by aristocratic conspiracy.

Czar Nicholas II and his entire family, 1918.
> The family was taken hostage and eventually shot and buried in unmarked graves to end the rule of Czars in Russia.

Mahatma Gandhi, 1948
> Shot at point blank range by Nathuram Godse in a well-planned conspiracy of multiple members.

Dr. Martin Luther King Jr., 1968
> A Civil Rights leader trying to abolish racial discrimination in the United States was assassinated by James Earl Ray, a segregationist.

Anwar Sadat, President of Egypt, 1981
> Having signed a Peace Treaty with Israel shot by Khalid Islambouli.

Benazir Bhutto, Former Prime Minister of Pakistan, 2007
> Female seeking re-election as Prime Minister, killed by car bomb.

Osama bin Laden, Terrorist Leader, 2011
> Assassinated by US Navy Seals in a surprise attack of his compound in Pakistan authorized by U.S. President, Barack Obama.

Take for example, Julius Caesar at the peak of his power.

Julius Caesar looked Brutus in the eye as the knife went into him and uttered the words as he fell: "Et tu, Brute!" (And you, Brutus!)

Does History repeat itself? We shall see.

There are so many examples in history of assassinations to gain power that it serves little purpose to cite them all when most fit the Julius Caesar example for instant change. While writing this book aboard ship in February 2012, there was an assassination attempt of Vladimir Putin in Russia who survived where the two assassins were caught and await their penalty.

Sometimes they are triggered by attempting to rid the world of someone too powerful like the unsuccessful attempts to kill Adolf Hitler and other times by those who inherit power just by their position of residing in their current position of second in command.

Is second in command a license to kill?

In the case of Julius Caesar the murder was committed in public that some claim as many as sixty senators were in attendance. The hand of Brutus and the bloody knife and so many witnesses are the evidence. A well planned murder leaving no evidence like that of President John F. Kennedy in 1963 will be a more difficult murder to solve.

The classic case of a conspiracy gone wrong is that of Rasputin. He just wouldn't die and made the conspirators a nervous wreck until he finally succumbed, days later.

CHAPTER II

THE HARD LESSONS
OF POLITICS

The 1956 Election

John F. Kennedy learned from his experience when nominated as a Vice Presidential candidate for Adlai Stevenson in the 1956 Democratic Convention that vast preparation is necessary to be nominated and then elected for nationwide office.

Kennedy lost this vice president nomination to Estes Kefauver and learned that Kefauver already had so many of the delegates organized in his corner before Kennedy's nomination, that there was really no contest.

However, Kennedy turned this disaster into opportunity by sincerely thanking his supporters on nationwide television for his Vice Presidential nomination and for the first time became known from coast to coast. The public liked what they saw in this heretofore unknown young, handsome, and charismatic candidate.

The Democrats lost anyway in the 1956 election to President Eisenhower. Kennedy experienced the valuable lesson of surprise to lose to the well-organized Kefauver so he started immediately to prepare a surprise for the 1960 election by collecting delegates 4 years in advance of the next election.

CHAPTER III

LYNDON JOHNSON
IS ACCOSTOMED TO POWER

THE 1960 ELECTION

Lyndon Johnson the very popular Democratic Senate Majority Leader had aspirations of running for President with the support of so many US Senators, that had told him that he could count on their support.

By comparison, Kennedy realized that delegates and governor's from each state are far more useful than senators at the Democratic Convention to secure the nomination.

By the time Johnson realized how many delegates Kennedy had promised to him he lashed out to those around him his true feelings.

"It was the goddamdest thing." He said with mournful relish, "here was this young whippersnapper . . . 'malaria-ridden yallah . . . sickly, sickly." Cross, p. 70.

Robert Kennedy, Jack's campaign, manager advised Jack not to even consider Johnson on the Democratic Ticket. He felt the man too powerful with too many connections, some even with Texas oil and underworld characters.

Sam Rayburn a mentor to Senator Johnson initially advised Johnson not to seek the Vice Presidency as he already had the second most powerful position in our government as Senate Majority Leader.

Bobby Baker, Lyndon Johnson's political advisor most always by his side advised Lyndon that we must convince Sam Rayburn that Vice President is a good idea. Eventually Sam Rayburn supported the idea.

Not only does the vice president preside over the senate but you will be sitting in the cat bird's seat for the most powerful position in the world.

Given Jack Kennedy's health, it should only be a matter of time.

In a surprise telephone call to John F. Kennedy from Phil Graham editor of the Washington Post.

"Young man, this is Phil Graham, I just want to say one thing to you. Don't tear something apart that you can never put it back together again." Cross, p.78.

What does Phil Graham mean? A Kennedy-Johnson ticket? Of course, such action would rid the Johnson attacks on Kennedy's deteriorating poor health and pick up the Texas delegates and much of the south as well.

Why would the most powerful Democrat who could bury Kennedy by continuing to make public his medical condition agree to be Vice President?

The obvious answer is because Johnson knew the seriousness of Kennedy's sickness could likely have him die in office, making the Vice-President President. In this scenario, Vice President is the fastest route to the Presidency when the President suffers from Addison's disease. Why not just wait it out?

"Johnson's mentor was Sam Rayburn, speaker of the house, who made it his business to contact Tip O'Neil saying, "If Kennedy wants Johnson for vice-president then he has nothing else he can do but to be on the ticket." Mathews, p. 281.

O'Neil met Jack outside Chasen's Restaurant in Hollywood, and told Kennedy what Rayburn had said, that Johnson would accept the Vice Presidency if offered, and gave him Johnson's phone number.

"It was a case of grasping the nettle." Schlesinger wrote in his journal July 15, 1960. Ibid, p.282

"Whether Johnson had played tough to try and secure the Presidential nomination for himself was no deterrent to running as Jack's Vice President." Ibid.

Johnson's arm twisting political career, keeping of file of gotcha on each of his, opponents and enemies, (their sexual orientation and philandering and foibles, etc.) will eventually pay off big.

Knowing J. Edgar Hoover has a file on him. Johnson kept a file on Hoover and his gay lover.

Make no mistake, Lyndon B. Johnson relishes power and thrives on power!

His biographers in researching his life come to the same conclusion. Johnson uses power as intimidation to those with less power.

CHAPTER IV

The Kennedy / Johnson Democratic Ticket

1960

History shows us that Lyndon Johnson accepted Jack's offer of Vice President on the Democratic Ticket in 1960.

Kennedy's Addison's Disease, is a rare chronic endocrine disorder, where the adrenal glands do not produce sufficient steroid hormones causing abdominal pain and weakness, low blood pressure with the possibility of coma.

Certainly Addison's Disease was a contributing factor in Johnson accepting the nomination of Vice President.

In the campaign Lyndon worked hard and delivered Texas and many southern states to Kennedy. Together Jack and Lyndon seemed to be a good team working together and got elected.

After Jack was inaugurated, the changes in Lyndon's status became apparent. Lyndon seemed to be pushed aside rather than admired. The Harvard crew tolerated his presence but gave little or no respect to his opinions.

John Patrick Roach Jr.

Johnson's name became a joke around the White House. He was the brunt of much humour as they made fun of his awkwardness.

Lyndon on the other hand dwelled in the knowledge of Jack's Addison's disease and many health problems. All he had to do as Vice President was wait until Kennedy's health does him in, to become the next President of the United States. Some thought Johnson was sitting in the cat bird's seat just waiting to be President.

Johnson, not appreciated at home as much as he would like, took quite a few trips out of the country and overseas as Vice President representing the President.

On many of these trips, he felt good about himself again.

CHAPTER V

CAMELOT

During his first term, Jack had many relapses of Addison's disease and other sickness that were intentionally kept from the public. After all Jack Kennedy was in so much physical pain that cortisone shots were often needed to help him function, yet he didn't die. He survived them all and lived on to become not only our youngest President to date but one of our greatest for peace.

Most everyone remembers John F. Kennedy's inspiring words in his inaugural address upon taking office.

"Ask not what your country can do for you; ask what you can do for your country".

President Kennedy established the Peace Corps, where many Americans volunteered to serve overseas and around the world helping nations overcome poverty.

When United States was threatened my missiles capable of being launching from Cuba only 90 miles away he forced the Soviet Union to back down and remove all missile launching equipment from Cuba. By doing so he averted a nuclear confrontation with the Soviet Union.

JFK did not live to see the United States landing on the moon, but he is certainly credited with starting such an ambitious successful project.

Most notable of Kennedy's accomplishments for Peace was the signing of the Nuclear Limited Test Ban Treaty.

Jack Kennedy with so many outstanding accomplishments for peace was an extremely popular President. Jack, with his beautiful First Lady Jacqueline became known by admirers as a creating a Camelot as the song in the Broadway play stated:

"Don't let it be known, that there once was a spot; that for one shining moment, that was known as Camelot."

Nearing the end of Jack's first term, there was no real question in Lyndon Johnson's mind that Kennedy would be re-elected. If Lyndon Johnson were not to be selected Vice President for the second term, the hope of Lyndon's presidential aspirations would be lost.

Kennedy was successful in defeating Adlai Stevenson at the Democratic convention, who was backed by Eleanor Roosevelt. With Lyndon Johnson, accepting his offer of vice-president, John F. Kennedy becomes the Democrats choice to run for President against Richard Nixon.

Pitted against Richard Nixon the Republican candidate in the Presidential Race of 1960, Kennedy used the same tactics of face to face meetings with delegates and governors and won again, this time to become President of the United States of America.

Kennedy wasted no time as the current President in making personal visits to delegates and getting to know them one on one.

Jacqueline and President John F. Kennedy always drew a crowd during our era of Camelot. *Photo by Abbie Rowe, courtesy of John F. Kennedy Presendential Library and Museum, Boston.*

JFK and children Caroline and John Jr, in the Oval Office.
16 October, 1962

Photo by Cecil Stoughton, Courtesy of John F. Kennedy
Presidential Library and Museum, Boston.

The Kennedy Children, Caroline and John, entertaining President, John F. Kennedy, in the oval office. Courtesy of John F. Kennedy Presidential Library and Museum, Boston.

JFK Press Conference, Public Domain

CHAPTER VI

J. Edger Hoover

The Nation's Top Cop

If you are going to succeed as the top cop, you had better have dossiers on any person that can threaten you. This, J. Edgar Hoover accomplished.

Our Democracy depends on a system of Checks and Balances. The President of the United States appoints an Attorney General who is J. Edgar Hoover's boss. Hoover, who had worked under nine Presidents, had a secret file on each.

In 1919 Attorney General Mitchell Palmer, in the Administration of Woodrow Wilson, named hard working and rising star J. Edgar Hoover the first director of General Intelligence Division of the Justice Department.

During the Harding years the bureau of investigation did much to break up illegal bootlegging operations and built files of the administrations enemies.

During the administration of Calvin Coolidge, Hoover got a lot of favourable press when he investigated and solved the Charles Lindberg Kidnapping Case.

During President Herbert Hoover's administration and the Franklin Delano Roosevelt administration many criminals were caught, tried and convicted.

Famous criminals were brought to Justice. Baby Face Nelson, John Dillinger and Pretty Boy Floyd, just to name a few.

In 1935 the name of J. Edgar Hoover's office reporting to the Justice Department was officially changed to the Federal Bureau of Investigation, hereinafter, FBI.

With the surprise attack on Pearl Harbor in 1941, the FBI was given more power. President Roosevelt authorized the FBI to use wire taps, censorship of publications that could contain secret information and hidden bugs in suspects' homes, offices, hotel rooms, etc.

Harry Truman became President in 1945 and ended World War II with two Atomic Bombs causing Japan to surrender. Truman did not like the idea of bugs and electronic surveillance of United States citizens and told J. Edgar Hoover as much.

Hoover's efforts turned to the elimination of communism in the United States and suspected Soviet spies were infiltrating our government. The FBI had many informants and lists of possible communists.

By now you can see the unrestricted and unchecked power that J. Edgar Hoover both gained and used.

Eisenhower with his vice President Nixon followed the Truman administration and both were supportive of the FBI. Hoover knew this and provided information to both that was used in getting them elected.

In 1960 President John F. Kennedy defeated Nixon and appointed his brother, Robert Kennedy, Attorney General.

Even before the 1960 election, Hoover's file on John Kennedy showed his relationship with Inga Arvad, a Danish beauty that during World War II was also close to Adolf Hitler.

Hoover let Kennedy know: "If the public found out about his relationship with Inga Arvad, Kennedy's political career would be over. Only Hoover could make this story public and only Hoover could keep it a secret. Just a few days after Kennedy was sworn in as President, he reappointed Hoover as Director of the FBI." Striessgurth, p. 91.

Hoover thought Martin Luther King Jr. was getting too powerful and warned President Kennedy that he suspected he was a communist and commenced the wiretapping to build a case against King.

John F. Kennedy knew that Hoover had a file containing records of his many infidelities. If Kenned6y were re-elected in 1964, Hoover would certainly be retired in less than 18 months at the mandatory retirement age of 70 and most likely be replaced by his boss, Attorney General, Bobby Kennedy.

Kennedy was also aware of Hoover's sexual orientation, a potential scandal that could erupt at any time.

Hoover's access to the White House was diminished when Jack Kennedy told him he no longer has direct access and must go through the Attorney General, Robert Kennedy.

Hoover was irritated by this as he saw his boss Robert Kennedy as not even living up to the FBI dress code.

Hoover as the head of the FBI, Hoover would have the resources to: If corrupt, be a superstar co-conspirator or a superstar cover-up specialist.

Ironically, he most likely became a superstar of both the assassination and the cover-up.

If a co-conspirator with Vice President Johnson, The Vice President becomes President and J. Edgar Hoover keeps his job at least until Robert Kennedy is assassinated.

Curt Gentry, a Hoover Biographer states:

"On November 23, the Day after the assassination, Hoover sent the White House the FBI's "preliminary inquiry" into the death of President Kennedy, together with a summary memorandum containing some of the information the Bureau had on Oswald." Gentry p. 543.

"Officially the FBI was now on record as stating that Lee Harvey Oswald, acting alone, was the assassin of the late President. Having made up his mind on this point-solving the case, in effect, in less than 24 hours—Hoover never changed it, no matter how much the evidence might indicate otherwise." Ibid.

A head of the FBI, Hoover is quick to name Oswald as the assassin and Ruby as the murderer of Oswald.

Why is that so believable?

Because the population saw Ruby murder Oswald "live" on television. Hoover went on to proclaim that Oswald acted alone, and there was no conspiracy involved.

President Lyndon Johnson succeeded Kennedy and announced that Hoover's required retirement at age 70 has been waived.

"Hoover himself still worked against civil rights in his own way. He continued the surveillance of Martin Luther King Jr. When King was nominated for the Nobel Prize in 1964, Hoover exploded in anger.

He began a campaign to slander King's name among people who supported him. He released tapes of King's private conversations and private activities. The tapes worried many of King's aids and disrupted the activities of the Southern Christian Leadership Conference (SCLC), founded by King in 1957, who became its first President.

FBI agents sent a letter to King, promising to expose his actions if he did not disappear from public life." Streissguth, p. 105.

"Microphone surveillance of King's hotel room produced what the bureau called "Entertainment," sounds of partying, drinking and engaging in sexual relations. Now Hoover had another reason for hating King: King is a tom cat." he told his aids, "with obsessive degenerate sexual urges." Powers, p.417.

Hoover pursued his investigations of Martin Luther King Jr. to the point where he did everything possible to disparage King to those trying to honor King. In essence, this is a case where there should be no question of Hoover's willingness to involve himself in a conspiracy to destroy Dr. Martin Luther King Jr. as detailed by his biographer, Curt Gentry p. 567-576.

Some of the tapes were given to President Johnson who used parts of them to entertain his close friends.—"since not long after their visit the President of the United States began entertaining selected White House guests by playing portions of the King tapes." Ibid, p. 570

Hoover referring to King as a "notorious liar" caused King to respond.

"King released a statement suggesting that Hoover had faltered under the awesome burden, complexities and responsibilities of his office."

King later demanded a meeting with Hoover.

"Hoover's advisors counsel him against seeing King and William Sullivan took it upon himself to make relevant copies of Kings' sexual activities to accompany the following letter:

King, look into your heart. You know you are a complete fraud and a greater liability to all us Negroes. White people in this country have enough frauds of their own but I am sure they don't have one at this time that is anywhere near your equal. You are no clergyman and you know it. Repeat that you are a colossal and an evil vicious one at that."....

King, like all frauds your end is approaching. You could have been our greatest leader .... but you are done ...

The American Public, the church organizations that you have been helping—Protestants, Catholics and Jews will know you for what you are—an evil beast, So will others who have backed you, you are done, King, there is only one thing left for you to do. You know what that is. You have just 34 days in which to do (the exact number has been selected for a specific reason, it has definite practical significance} You are done. There is but one way out for you. You better take it before your filthy fraudulent self is barred in the nation". Powers, p 420.

April 4th, 1968, Dr. Martin Luther King Jr. was assassinated at a Memphis motel and minutes later confirmed dead.

June 6, 1968 Robert Kennedy was assassinated at the Ambassador Hotel in Los Angeles, CA.

Both assassinations were committed by a gunman with a background as outrageous as Lee Harvey Oswald.

Finally, after 48 years of service while still serving as FBI Chief, J. Edgar Hoover was found dead of natural causes the morning of May 2, 1972 at the age of 77.

Henel Grandy, Hoover's secretary, immediately destroyed his confidential files that he kept in his office as he instructed she do upon his death.

J. Edgar Hoover, FBI Director meeting with his
superiors, President John F. Kennedy and Attorney
General Robert F. Kennedy. *Courtesy of John F.
Kennedy Presidential Library and Museum, Boston.*

J. Edgar Hoover
FBI Director.

Photo: FBI Public Domain.

CHAPTER VII

PLANNING FOR A SECOND TERM

Nearing the end of Jack's first term, there was no real question in Lyndon Johnson's mind that Kennedy would be re-elected. If Lyndon Johnson were not to be selected Vice President for the second term, the hope of Lyndon's presidential aspirations would be lost.

Kennedy anticipated challenges from both Lyndon Johnson who by 1964 will have collected damaging evidence concerning Kennedy's Addison's Disease and poor health, to propose that he is unfit to hold office for another four years.

Three and a half years of visiting Governors of each state and delegates from each state personally would certainly pay off, when during the fourth year Lyndon Johnson with all his support from Senators as Majority Leader counted too little too late, as Kennedy pretty much had a majority of the Governors and delegates of each state already committed. Johnson was furious, but too late!

IT IS NOW TIME FOR JOHNSON TO TAKE ACTION.

Kennedy must be taken out!

What are the chances for success?

Let's look at the history of trying to assassinate U.S. Presidents that follows.

Vice President Lyndon B. Johnson and President
John F. Kennedy. *Photo courtesy of John F. Kennedy
Presidential Library and Museum, Boston.*
Photo by Abbie Rowe

CHAPTER VIII

Attempts to kill U.S. Presidents

1835	Andrew Jackson	Unsuccessful
	Richard Lawrence found guilty, declared insane and institutionalized.	
1865	Abraham Lincoln	Successful
	John Wilkes Booth shoots Lincoln at Ford's Theatre.	
1881	James A. Garfield	Successful
	Charles J. Geiteau shot Garfield and was hanged 9 months later.	
1901	William McKinely	Successful
	Leon Czolgosz electrocuted 13 months later.	
1912	Theodore Roosevelt	Unsuccessful
	John F. Schrank shot Teddy, captured and found insane, Teddy, never had the bullet removed.	
1950	Harry S. Truman	Unsuccessful
	Oscar Collazo and Griselio. Torresola, shot. Collazo got life sentence.	
1963	John F. Kennedy	Successful
	November 22nd, 1963.	

NOTES:

Attempts to assassinate Franklin D. Roosevelt in 1933 <u>before he became President</u> by Giuseppe Zangara killing Chicago Mayor Anton Cermak. Zangara was found guilty of murder and executed on March 20, 1933.

Unsuccessful

Attempts to Assassinate George H.W. Bush in 1993 with a car bomb, while not in office and visiting Kuwait University were foiled by Kuwaiti Security. The 16 members of the plot were arrested with the bomb in evidence.

Unsuccessful

A Presidential Candidate for the Democratic Party in 1968 intending to challenge incumbent President Lyndon Johnson was U.S. Senator Robert F. Kennedy a younger brother of John F. Kennedy. He was assassinated on June 5, 1968 by Sirhan Sirhan with four bullets.

Successful

Source. Los Angeles Times Data Desk, 2013.

CHAPTER IX

THE TIME IS NOW SCENERIO

PLANNING A CONSPIRACY FOR ASSASSINATIONS
With two objectives:
Dead Victims and leaving No Evidence of Conspiracy.

SELECT A VICTIM.

FIND AN ASSASSIN # 1 with explainable notorious past.

FIND ASSASSIN # 2 with notorious past.

FIND ASSASSIN # 3 with prejudice.

FIND ASSASSIN # 4 for back-up situations.

DETERMINE DATE AND TIME FOR ASSASSINATION.

PROVIDE TIP TO POLICE OF ASSASSINS ESCAPE ROUTE.

ASSASSIN # 1 ARRESTED.

IMPLEMENT ASSASSIN # 2 KILLING ASSASSIN # 1 WHILE UNDER ARREST.

IMPLEMENT POLICE CAPTURE OF ARMED ASSASSIN # 2.

RESULT:

DEAD VICTIMS WITH ALL EVIDENCE OF CONSPIRACY ELIMANATED.

INVESTIGATION AND REPORT CITING NO EVIDENCE OF CONSPIRACY.

MASTERMINDS OF CONSPIRACY FREE TO BENEFIT AND DO AS THEY PLEASE.

Jack Ruby shoots Lee Harvey Oswald. FBI photo.

Jack Ruby Mug Shots, FBI photo.

Lee Harvey Oswald, who assassinated President
Kennedy, and then was himself killed two days later.
Unknown photographer. Public domain. The 1960s
Schmoop.com

CHAPTER X

LEE HARVEY OSWALD

Born October 18, 1939 to Marguerite Oswald, whose husband died of a heart attack two months before his birth, leaving a widow with three sons, John from a previous marriage and Robert and now, Lee Harvey Oswald.

Marguerite struggled financially during the early years and remarried to Edwin A. Ekdahl in 1945, who served as a surrogate father to Oswald until their divorce three years later.

Previously known as a good student who preferred solitude to friendship and social activities, Oswald started playing hooky and was absent from school so often that it was reported to the authorities. He often had to change schools. By 1953 in the 7th grade he was truant so often that out of a period of 64 schooldays he only attended less than 16.

Lee Oswald's rebellious attitude continued through high school until he decided to quit school at age 17 and join the U.S. Marine Corps. He enlisted four days after his eligibility and reported for duty at the Marine Corps Recruit Depot in San Diego, CA., on October 26th, 1956.

During his recruit training, Lee qualified as "Sharpshooter" with the M1 rifle, a medal greater than "Marksman" and less than

"Expert." While serving his term in the Marines, Lee Oswald was known to be a loner. He was not well liked by fellow Marines.

Lee became interested in Socialism, and the Russian language. He referred to himself as a Marxist and started to lose interest in the Marine Corps.

Lee Oswald received an "undesirable discharge" from the Marine Corps reserve based on his often expressed intent to renounce his U.S. citizenship to become a citizen of the Soviet Union.

Within weeks, Oswald boarded a ship bound for La Harve, France. Upon arrival, he flew to London and on to Helsinki, Finland, where he hoped to get a visitors' Visa to Russia.

The best Oswald could do in Finland was getting a 6 day tourist Visa to visit Russia, so he immediately did so. Two of his six day pass were wasted on the train ride to Moscow.

Once in Moscow, he was assigned a tourist guide that watched over him as they toured the city. He let the guide know that he desired to become a citizen of the U.S.S.R., and asked her to help him. She said she would and reported this information to the authorities.

Oswald had some interviews, even on his 6th day and was hopeful he could get an extension on his Visa.

On the 7th day he received a message that his visa was no longer valid and he must be out of the country in two hours.

Oswald slit his wrist and was found by his tour guide and rushed to the hospital and committed to the psychological ward for observation. Shortly thereafter he was told that his visa is extended and he should report to a job waiting for him in Minsk, as well as an apartment.

The job involved cutting sheet metal and the apartment was above the Russian standard overlooking the river, so Oswald was pleased.

At a dance in Minsk, Oswald met Marina and asked her to dance. She was 18 at the time and he was 24. They got along well and after a few dates they fell in love and were married.

Lee and Marina Oswald enjoyed their life together in the summer and fall especially in the outdoors. The winters were quite harsh but they had the opera and symphony.

Eventually, it occurred to Oswald that he was making good money but there was little opportunity to spend it. He would like to take Marina to the Black Sea Resorts in the Crimea, but that seems to be reserved for the Communists.

Eventually, he became disillusioned and discussed returning to the United States with Marina, with her as an immigrant and him as asking for the return of his Passport.

Oswald wrote a letter to Texas Governor John Connelly, asking him to have his military records cleaned up and to make sure no charges will be filed against him upon his desired return to the U.S.

John Connelly forwarded Oswald's letter to the Navy Department in an effort to help.

In the meantime, Marina now pregnant with baby June Oswald meant that Oswald needed permission from both the Soviet Government and the U.S. Government for the three of them to enter the United States.

Life in Fort Worth, Texas was not easy for the couple. They had few relatives and made new friends in the Russian Community willing to help, but jobs were hard to find and Lee was dissatisfied with himself and they argued a lot.

They eventually moved to Dallas where Lee got a job, then New Orleans. He referred to himself as either Secretary or Director of, "The Fair Play for Cuba Committee," then, Mexico City, where he tried to get a Visa to visit Cuba unsuccessfully. Finally, Oswald became so disillusioned that once again he returned to Dallas and filed for unemployment.

Mrs. Ruth Paine, separated from her husband and living in Irving, Texas, had invited Marina and her baby June to live with her during the three months of Lee's travelling and job search and return from Mexico City. Lee Oswald was certainly having financial problems during this time.

Ruth Paine was not only caring for them but was trying to help Lee Oswald get a job in Dallas.

Ruth Paine, through friends heard of an employment opening at the Texas School Book Depository in Dallas and informed Marina. Oswald was interviewed and got the job starting October 16, 1963. The job was filling book orders at $1.25 per hour.

Oswald was happy to have a job feeling he could get a better job someday from this one, but by working, he made his family and few friends happy.

He visited his wife In Irving, Texas, every weekend but one, since his employment at the Texas School Book Depository.

On November 18th, the Presidential Motorcade route was established and published in the Dallas newspapers on November 19th.

On November 21st, Oswald returned to Ruth Paine's home to see his wife and daughter and pick up a package of wrapped up Curtin rods. He played with his daughter and asked his pregnant wife to move to Dallas with him, and she refused. He stayed overnight and left the next morning with the package.

One day later on Nov. 22nd, 1963, President Kennedy was assassinated and Texas Governor Connelly was wounded in a Dallas motorcade as it passed the Texas School Book Depository.

On Nov. 24th, Lee Harvey Oswald was murdered on live Television, for all the world to see, by Jack Ruby, a local Dallas Night Club owner.

Jack Ruby was taken into custody by the Dallas Police Department, desiring to be known as the patriot that killed President Kennedy's assassin.

Regarding Lee Harvey Oswald motivation for this assassination the Warren Commission Report concludes:

"Many factors were undoubtedly involved in Oswald's motivation for the assassination, and the commission does not believe that it can ascribe to him any one motive or group of motives. It is apparent, however, that Oswald was moved by an overriding hostility to his environment.

He does not appear to have been able to establish meaningful relationships with other people. He was perpetually discontented with the world around him.

Long before the assassination he expressed his hatred for American society and acted in protest against it. Oswald's search for what he conceived to be the perfect society was doomed from the start. He sought for himself a place in history—a role as "the great man" who would be recognized as having been in advance of his times.

His commitment to Marxism and communism appears to have been another important factor in his motivation. He also had demonstrated a capacity to act decisively and without regard to the consequences when such action would further the aims of the moment. Out of these and the many other factors which may have molded the character of Lee Harvey Oswald there emerged a man capable of assassinating President Kennedy." Warren, p. 423

Without any accomplishments, Oswald wondered why his self acclaimed greatness was never recognized?

Jacqueline and President John F. Kennedy arrival in
Dallas on Air Force One, November 22, 1963.

*Photo courtesy of John F, Kennedy Memorial Library
and Museum, Boston, MA.*

CHAPTER XI

THE ASSASSINATION

Brought to you live on television. Millions became instant eyewitnesses to the President recoiling from shots to his head, slumping over onto his loving wife Jacqueline, as the open roof limo picked up speed and headed toward Parkland Hospital.

Vice President Johnson's limo and others in the motorcade followed the Presidential limo to Parkland Hospital.

Lee Harvey Oswald was stopped by Officer Tippet while suspiciously walking too fast from his home where he spoke to Oswald from the police car. Unsatisfied with some of Oswald's answers, Officer Tippet got out of the car, walked over to Oswald and was shot four times and killed by Oswald.

Oswald sought to hide in a dark movie theatre without paying. The ticket person called Dallas police and Oswald was apprehended, taken into custody and charged with the murder of Officer Tippet.

Oswald who works in the Texas School Book Depository along the route taken by the Presidential motorcade, became the prime suspect in the assassination of President Kennedy, although he was not yet charged.

CHAPTER XII

CHOREOGRAPHY

PARKLAND HOSPITAL

"O'Donnell was not only Kennedy's top aid on the trip, but had been Johnson's main contact person at the White House. As long as Kennedy was alive, Johnson wanted to avoid appearing overeager to assume the Presidency." Gillon, Chapter 6.

Ken O'Donnell advised Johnson to return to Washington.

"It was a psychological standoff: O'Donnell would not say that Kennedy was dead and Johnson would not leave the Hospital until he did. If Johnson had been more secure and less paranoid about R.F.K., he would have been more decisive about assuming the reins of power." Ibid.

At approximatcly 1:00 pm President John F. Kennedy died at Parkland Hospital and twenty minutes later O'Donnell informed Johnson.

Technically at the moment of Kennedy's death Johnson became the President of the United States or is he not President until he takes the oath?

Scholars to this day have not resolved this question.

The President's plane, Air Force One, awaits the entourage at Love Field in Dallas.

The new President Johnson did not want to wait to be sworn in back in Washington, but wanted to take the oath on Air Force One before takeoff with Kennedy's body on board as well, in the presence of Jacqueline Kennedy and members of the Kennedy staff.

Johnson, placed a call to Attorney General, Bobby Kennedy for advice on how to accomplish the swearing in. Bobby, already informed of his brother's death by J. Edgar Hoover did his best to comply with Johnson's wishes and concluded, anyone can swear you in.

Johnson chose Sarah Hughes a person he recommended to Robert Kennedy to appoint to a Federal Judgeship. RFK informed Johnson that at her age of 65, she is too old. Johnson was left with the task of informing her. Weeks later, House Speaker Sam Rayburn met with Robert Kennedy and the Justice Department made Sarah Hughes a Federal Judge.

Judge Sarah Hughes arrived on board and was ready to administer the oath and Johnson said, "Mrs. Kennedy wants to be here. We'll wait for her."

"Johnson asked O'Donnell to see if Mrs. Kennedy would stand with him. O'Donnell who was trying to move things along, still fearing that the Dallas Police would try to prevent the plane from taking off, was shocked by the request."

"You can't do that, Mr. President!" The poor little kid has had enough for one day, to sit here and hear the oath that she heard a few years ago! You just can't do that. Mr. President! Johnson however, insisted."

"Although sensitive to her private suffering, LBJ also understood the symbolic power of having the first Lady standing by his side."

Still other historians take a different point of view of these few intense hours.

"In the hour that passed while he waited at Parkland and then at Air Force One, he could not resist calling Robert Kennedy to ask for a legal opinion on taking the oath. After all, the president's brother was Attorney General. There was absolutely no need for such an invasive and direct reminder of the personal loss Robert Kennedy had suffered. After three years of torment from John Kennedy's brother. Johnson had to rub it in." McClellan p. 212.

Johnson's insistence that Jackie Kennedy stand beside him while he takes the oath, McClellan describes as follows:

"Again, in terribly boorish and unacceptable poor taste, he insisted she be there beside him." Ibid.

November 22nd, 1963, "Throughout the day Johnson carefully choreographed the images that America saw of him. He allowed a photographer to record the swearing in on *Air Force One,* and insisted that the press be granted access to his arrival at *Andrews Air Force Base*, later that evening.

On Saturday, he made sure a photographer snapped pictures of his meetings with key members of the Kennedy Cabinet." Gillon, p.100

The result of all these well planned photo releases to the media enabled the distraught American Public to realize that our government is still operational, and guided by the new President with the advisors of the Kennedy cabinet ready to support him.

Minutes after the Swear—in Ceremony. *Courtesy of the John F. Kennedy Library and Museum, Boston.*

CHAPTER XIII

PRESIDENT LYNDON JOHNSON

On November 22nd, 1963, President Lyndon Banes Johnson became President of the United States of America as the shots rang out in his home state of Texas, ending the life of John F. Kennedy and America's vision of Camelot.

Most American's can remember where they were at the shocking moment they heard the tragic news that our beloved President John F. Kennedy was dead.

For those of you who believe in woman's intuition, Jacqueline Kennedy was not of the opinion that the mafia, Cubans or other aliens shot her husband, she concluded through logic and reason who the culprit was, that hired the assassins.

President Johnson was sworn in on Air Force One, the same plane returning to Washington, DC with Jacqueline Kennedy and the remains of her husband, the former President of the United States of America.

Jacqueline Kennedy returned to the White House with family members the evening of November 22 for a very concentrated next morning of funeral preparations. The decision was made for a closed casket as the damage to Kennedy's head was too severe, and the casket was placed in the East Room of the White House on

November 23rd, for the entire Saturday for the visits of dignitaries, former Presidents and people of State.

On Sunday, the casket was moved to the Rotunda of the Capital Building to lie in state and be visible to the public before the funeral the next morning on November 25th, 1963, when the casket was lowered and John F. Kennedy was buried at Arlington Cemetery.

November 22nd, 23rd, 24th and 25th, in 1963, from a smiling President and his beautiful First Lady getting off Air Force One in Dallas, to the return to Washington, D.C., the same day on the same Air Force One, to the grief of the entire nation. The horse drawn caisson of the funeral processions to the final resting place of our beloved President John F. Kennedy on the sloping hill below the former mansion of General Robert E. Lee, (see, Eternal Flame, on this book's cover.) the entire funeral choreographed by Jacqueline Kennedy intended to be reminiscent of the funeral of Abraham Lincoln.

Camelot is over and there is an eternal flame that marks the spot where Jacqueline Kennedy who died in 1994 is laid to rest next to her husband John F. Kennedy and their two infant children.

The new President on November 27th, obligated to find and bring to justice the murderers involved established a commission to investigate. "The President's Commission on the Assassination of President John F. Kennedy," also known as the Warren Commission, headed by Chief Justice Earl Warren.

In Updegrove's book, *Indominatable Will, LBJ in the Presidency,* the author refers to LBJ's quest for power on page 117 as follows:

"That Lyndon Johnson relished power is undeniable. He spent almost his whole adult life working toward its pursuit, retention and consolidation, and exercised it with reflexive ease. Indeed, he basked in the power of the presidency almost imperially."

Both as Vice President and as President, Johnson was fearful of two scandals either of which could erupt, expose him and have him removed from office. The first called the Billy Sol Estes Scandal involving Johnson's involvement in illegal activities and the second, the Bobby Baker Scandal either of which could have him removed from office but both would no longer attract the greatest audience.

With the Assassination of President Kennedy, the press lost its interest in pursuing Johnson Scandals, to focus on the assassination.

The author goes on to cite examples of Johnson's mastery of power throughout the book, and does point out Johnson's sensitive feelings of not being recognized as an important contributor in solving the Cuban Missile Crisis. Updegrove, p. 58.

He quotes LBJ, "They had thirty-seven meetings and I was in thirty-six of them. I missed one." p.58. Bobby Kennedy's book *Thirteen Days* "does not highlight in any way, LBJ's role." *ibid.*

Almost a year later on September 24, 1964 the 888 page Warren Commission report was delivered to President Lyndon B. Johnson that concluded:

1. Lee Harvey Oswald fired the shots that killed Kennedy and wounded Texas Governor Connelly.

2. Jack Ruby killed Oswald.

3. Government agents captured and jailed Ruby. Who died of accelerated cancer.

FACT: The Warren Report was unable to prove conspiracy.

If you believe the Warren Report you must be pretty gullible. It satisfies nothing except the ignorant belief that if something is in print, it must be true. The only truth is, everyone including perhaps the culprit in 1964 is dead. The culprits did in fact, get away with murder.

At the press conference, Oswald, himself said: "I'm just the patsy." Patsy for whom was never answered.

Secondly, The Warren Report is pretty much a mirror image of the FBI report provided by J Edgar Hoover.

Thirdly, The person who had the most to gain by the assassination of President Kennedy, is the very same person who commissioned the Warren report i.e, President Lyndon B. Johnson.

It is not a very satisfying result of the *The President's Commission on the Assassination of President John F. Kennedy.* Commissioned by none other than President Lyndon B. Johnson, himself, the person that had the most to gain from the assassination.

Tantamount to saying I ordered a book written that places blame without any consideration to who had the most to gain.

The upcoming anniversary, 50 years later on November 22nd, 2013, the public has apparently accepted that the case is closed.

Although, not everyone?

Certainly not me!

Jacqueline Kennedy next to Lyndon Johnson during his taking the Oath of Office on Air Force One. *Photo courtesy of John F. Kennedy Presidential Library and Museum, Boston*

Caisson leaving White House. *Photo by Abbie Rowe, courtesy of John F. Kennedy Library and Museum, Boston*

Casket being lowered at Arlington Cemetery, *Photo by Abbie Rowe, courtesy of John F. Kennedy Library and Museum, Boston*

CHAPTER XIV

JACK RUBY

Jacob Leon Rubenstein was born in Chicago, IL., on April 25, 1911 and is known to the world as Jack Ruby.

After serving in the Air Force, Ruby moves to Dallas in 1947.

Heavily in debt and cancer ridden, Jack Ruby is a perfect choice for a conspiracy to kill Oswald to prevent Oswald from talking.

Jack Ruby, a Dallas Night Club owner with a history of failed Night Clubs and shady dealings around Dallas was well known to the Police.

Ruby is five foot nine inches and 175 pounds, and is fond of carrying a big role of cash. He's got friends in the Mafia and in the police force. O'Reilly, p. 279.

Conspirators need only promise Ruby fame as a patriot and perhaps pay off his debts. There is no certainty that Ruby knew of his cancer before murdering Oswald but if he did, then knowing he had such a short time to live anyway, will admit the killing of Oswald and become a hero to some by avenging Jacqueline Kennedy's loss.

Ruby sought fame before he died.

If he were promised fame, he sure did get it.

No one questions the fact that: Ruby did murder Oswald on television before the entire nation.

When questioned by the Warren Commission on June 7, 1964 he is quoted as stating, "I have been used for a purpose." Kantor, P.18. He asked to be taken away from Dallas to Washington D.C., for a fair trial, "Take me to Washington D.C. and I will tell you all that I know. I cannot say anything here. I am the only one left that can tell you everything."

"The world will never know—nor would they believe—what took place here."

Ruby received the Death Penalty for his crime of shooting Oswald. In 1966 the death penalty was reversed by the Court of Appeals and he was granted a second trial.

Ruby tried to hang himself using sheets in his cell. He definitely wanted out of Dallas and is quoted as saying.

Ruby told his family that he was injected with cancer cells, he died a Parkland Hospital in Dallas on Jan. 3, 1967 from the effects of lung cancer at the age of 55.

If Jack Ruby had a secret that he wanted the world to know, it died with him.

CHAPTER XV

THE WARREN COMMISSION REPORT

"President Lyndon B. Johnson, by Executive Order No. 11130 dated November 29, 1963, created this Commission to investigate the assassination on November 29, 1963, of John Fitzgerald Kennedy, the 35th President of the United States." Warren, p.ix.

"The President directed the Commission to evaluate all the facts and circumstances surrounding the assassination and subsequent killing of the alleged assassin and report its findings to him". Ibid.

The official Warren Commission Report was delivered to President Lyndon B. Johnson on September 24, 1964, ten months after the assassination.

Relative to conspiracy the report concludes:

"that there is no credible evidence that Lee Harvey Oswald was part of a conspiracy to assassinate President Kennedy." Warren, p. 374.

"The Commission discovered no evidence that the Soviet Union or Cuba were involved in the assassination of President Kennedy." Ibid.

"Nor did he Commission's investigation of Jack Ruby produce any grounds for believing that Ruby's killing of Oswald was part of a conspiracy." Ibid.

"The evidence reviewed above identifies Lee Harvey Oswald as the assassin of President Kennedy and indicates that he acted alone in this event. Ibid, p.375.

CHAPTER XVI

PLANNING A CONSPIRACY FOR ASSASSINATION

With two objectives:

Dead Victim leaving No Evidence of Conspiracy.

SELECT A VICTIM.

FIND AN ASSASSIN # 1 FOR HIRE.

FIND ASSASSIN # 2 FOR HIRE.

FIND ASSASSIN # 3 FOR HIRE.

DETERMINE DATE AND TIME AND PLACE FOR ASSASSINATION.

PROVIDE TIP TO POLICE OF ASSASSINS ESCAPE ROUTE HAVE ASSASSIN # 1 ARRESTED.

IMPLEMENT ASSASSIN # 2 KILLING ASSASSIN # 1 WHILE UNDER ARREST.

A DEAD ASSASSIN #1, CAN NEVER SAY WHO HIRED HIM.

IMPLEMENT POLICE CAPTURE OF ARMED ASSASSIN # 2.

RESULT:

DEAD VICTIM WITH ALL EVIDENCE OF CONSPIRACY ELIMANATED.

INVESTIGATION AND REPORT CITING NO EVIDENCE OF CONSPIRACY.

MASTERMIND OF CONSPIRACY FREE TO BENEFIT AND DO AS HE PLEASES.

Sound Familiar?

WE THE CONSPIRATOR'S, DID IT SUCCESSFULLY ONCE!

LET'S DO IT AGAIN!

CHAPTER XVII

DR. MARTIN LUTHUR KING JR.

A leader in the non-violent African-American Civil Rights Movement who was inspired by Mahatma Gandhi's non-violent activism. Martin Luther King eventually visited India to see for himself. He returned to the United States realizing that such non-violent activism could be considered Civil Disobedience, and pursued this path even to the point of a March on Washington, D.C., where before a crowd in excess of 250,000 marchers he gave a most wonderful and idealistic speech known to the world as "I have a Dream."

Many honors were bestowed on this remarkable man. Among the most prominent honored are: Time, Person of the Year in 1963, and the Nobel Peace Prize in 1964.

President Kennedy was alerted to rumors concerning King's private life and offered these prophetic statements.

"King must sever his ties with Communists and be cautious about his infidelities." O'Reilly, p.181.

"You must be careful not to lose your cause. If they shoot you down, they'll shoot us down too. So be careful". Ibid.

John F. Kennedy was assassinated on November 22nd, 1963.

Martin Luther King was assassinated by James Earl Ray in Memphis, TN. in 1968 at the age of 39.

Since that time Martin Luther King Day has been declared a National Holiday and he has received the Presidential Medal of Freedom awarded by President Jimmy Carter in 1977.

After the FBI tracked down James Earl Ray and had him extradited from London, England to face trial in the United States, he was convicted and imprisoned.

The King family started their own investigation and came to the conclusion that James Earl Ray was a pawn in a much larger conspiracy to assassinate Martin Luther King Jr.

The Justice Department of the United States offered to investigate the King family's findings.

"I believe that we, the King family and myself, made a mistake. When the President refused to appoint an independent "truth and reconciliation commission," and instead offered a DOJ investigation, we should have said, "no thank you," and made it clear that we could not and would not cooperate with another "official" investigation attached to the very institutions of power, which we believed had participated in the heinous crime being investigated." Pepper, p. 262.

"We didn't take that position and I believe we were wrong." Ibid.

Dr. Martin Luther King Jr.
Photo by Nobel Foundation in Public Domain

CHAPTER XVIII

JAMES EARL RAY

Ray's biography reads like the story of a perpetual loser. He dropped out of school at age 15 and joined the Army and served in Germany. In 1949 he was convicted of a burglary in California. He got in trouble again in 1952 for armed robbery of a taxi driver and served 2 years in Illinois.

Criminal activity was becoming a way of life for James Earl Ray. Stealing money orders and forging them for cash was easy money for Ray until he got caught and served three years at Leavenworth Federal Penitentiary.

The history of petty crimes finally caught up to him. In an armed robbery of a Kroger store for only $120.00, he was sentenced to twenty years at Missouri State Prison. His repeated offenses garnered him the 20 year sentence. James Earl Ray escaped from prison in a bread truck.

He bounced around from city to city on the move until he settled in Puerto Vallarta, Mexico, where set himself up as a porn photographer, taking pictures of local prostitutes.

James Earl Ray didn't even last a month at this venture. He arrived in Puerto Vallarta on October 19th, 1967. When his prostitute girlfriend left him. He got discouraged and left Mexico by November 16th, 1967, arriving in Los Angeles the same day.

An avid segregationist, James Earl Ray joined the George Wallace Presidential Campaign with his quest to eventually move to Rhodesia where the white minority rules.

There is no question that James Earl Ray is a misfit in American Society but up to this point murder is not on his resume'.

At the time James Earl Ray was alleged to have assassinated Martin Luther King Jr., he claimed to be on his way to Rhodesia and was tracked down by the FBI in London, England, extradited, put on trial and convicted.

Ray was alleged to have rented a room on April 4, 1968, under a fictitious name, near the Lorraine Motel where King was staying and shot King from a bathroom window while balancing his rifle on the window ledge.

James Earl Ray, pleaded guilty in order to not get the death penalty which at that time was the electric chair in Tennessee. His guilty plea got him life in prison instead.

When Ray learned of the corruption of his defense lawyer he tried unsuccessfully to change his plea to not guilty.

Dexter King, the son of Martin Luther King Jr., visited James Earl Ray in prison, listened to his story and told him that he believed Ray did not kill his father and shook his hand.

Dr. William Pepper represented the King family in a wrongful death suit against Lloyd Jowers. The King family has since concluded that James Earl Ray had nothing to do with the assassination.

James Earl Ray died at the age of 70, while in prison on April 28, 1998.

PHOTO OF JAMES EARL RAY
FBI Photograph, Public Domain

PHOTO OF JAMES EARL RAY-WANTED POSTER

CHAPTER XIX

ROBERT F. KENNEDY

Robert F. Kennedy (Bobby) had advised his brother Jack not to consider Lyndon Johnson for Vice President on the ticket. In his planned role as protector of his brother Jack, Robert at the time did not have all the facts, only the belief, that Lyndon Johnson is motivated by POWER.

With the elections behind them, President John F. Kennedy, appointed his brother, Robert Kennedy, as Attorney General and re-confirmed, J. Edgar Hoover as Director of the FBI, reporting to the Attorney General.

President Kennedy also advised Hoover to no longer contact him directly, but to go through his capable brother Robert for access to the President.

J. Edgar Hoover was quite taken back by this instruction as he considered Robert Kennedy a kid, who didn't even dress to the standards of the FBI, put his feet on the desk, disrespectful of government property and even brought his dog with him to FBI Headquarters where the dog peed on the floor.

Nearing 40 years of service as FBI Director, Hoover found taking orders from Robert Kennedy intolerable and spent most of his time avoiding the Attorney General

Photograph of Senator, Robert F. Kennedy
FBI Photo, Public Domain

"By the end of 1962, two disastrous decisions were made by the President and his brother. They had decided to dump Lyndon Johnson in the upcoming 1964 election and force the resignation of J. Edgar Hoover as Director of the FBI. Morrow, p.77.

"To Hoover, the thought of the Kennedy brothers forcing his resignation as head of the most powerful agency in the United States, was unthinkable." Ibid, p.78.

"One of them had to go. It would not be J. Edgar Hoover. He theorized that the FBI was responsible for all the country's internal security. As its patriarch, he was above common law. Aligned with his powerful Texas friends, he could command a potent political force that would keep him as director until he died, once the Kennedy's were removed from office." Ibid, p. 79.

With the assassination of John F. Kennedy in 1963, Robert had to regroup his thoughts as everything now must be re-evaluated.

He never liked Lyndon B. Johnson, who was now President and is expected to run again in 1968.

The TET Offensive in Viet Nam caused Lyndon to re-think his plan to run in for second term and back out by withdrawing his name from contention.

The Republican Party would probably nominate Nixon and the Democrat primary looked like Senator Eugene McCarthy would be favored.

On March 16th, 1967, Robert F, Kennedy declared his candidacy for the Presidency of the United States on the Democratic Ticket.

"Bobby, KNEW, the only practical course to avenge his brother's Death, was to attain the Presidency, and, again control the Justice Department." Morrow, p.120

Certainly J. Edgar Hoover understood the ramifications, if Bobby should become the Democratic candidate and win the election.

The rest is history.

Robert Kennedy a leading Presidential Candidate for the Democratic Party in 1968 intending to challenge the Republican nominee was assassinated on June 5, 1968 by Sirhan Sirhan with four bullets at close range in Los Angeles, CA.

Photo of Senator, Robert F. Kennedy
FBI Photograph, Public Domain

CHAPTER XX

SIRHAN SIRHAN

At the time of the Assassination of Robert Kennedy, Sirhan was working as a stable boy at Santa Anita Racetrack, in Arcadia, California. Born in Jerusalem and claiming to be a Palestinian with Jordanian citizenship.

Sirhan's family brought him to the United States at age 12.

He graduated from John Muir High School and attended Pasadena City College in California.

Sirhan's father had a difficult time adjusting to American society and often beat Sirhan until he became a victim of child abuse.

Sirhan's writings were used to show his dislike to Robert F. Kennedy. Various notes or scrawling state, "R.F.K. must die!" "Robert F. Kennedy must be assassinated before June 5th, 1968, and my determination to eliminate R.F.K. is becoming more and more of an unshakable obsession . . . He must be sacrificed for the cause of the poor exploited people."

"The prosecution was able to show that just two nights before the attack, on June 3rd, Sirhan was seen at the Ambassador Hotel, apparently attempting to learn the building's layout; evidence proved that he visited a gun range on June 4th. Further testimony by Alvin Clark, Sirhan's garbage collector, who claimed that Sirhan had told him a month before the attack of his intention to shoot Kennedy, seemed especially damning.

Sirhan's defense counsel, which included Attorney Grant Cooper, had hoped to demonstrate that the killing had been an impulsive act of a man with a mental deficiency, but when Judge Walker admitted into evidence pages from three of the journal notebooks that Sirhan had kept, it was clear that the murder was not only premeditated, but also "quite calculating and willful."

On March 3rd, 1969, in the Los Angeles courtroom, Cooper asked Sirhan directly if he had indeed shot Senator Kennedy. Sirhan replied immediately: "Yes, sir." but then stated that he did not bear any ill-will towards Kennedy.

Sirhan also testified that he had killed Kennedy "with 20 years of "malice aforethought." He explained in an interview with David Frost in 1989 that this referred to the time since the creation of the State of Israel. He has maintained since then that he has no memory of the crime, nor of making it.

A parole hearing for Sirhan is now scheduled every five years. On March 2, 2011, after 42 years in prison, Sirhan's 14th parole hearing was held, with Sirhan represented by his current attorney, William Frances Pepper. At his parole hearing, Sirhan testified that he continues to have no memory of the assassination nor of any details of his 1969 trial and confession.

Pepper also repeated the claim, that Sirhan's lawyers previously stated in the past, that Sirhan's mind was "programmed" and then "wiped" by an unknown conspiracy behind the assassination which is why Sirhan has no memory of the murder or of the aftermath. His parole was denied on the grounds that Sirhan still does not understand the full ramifications of his crime." Source Wikipedia 06/08/13.

Consensus: He appeared to be a self-appointed assassin who thought RFK was no good because he was helping the Jews. Or, was Sirhan any different than Oswald who claimed to be a "Patsy," or Ray who claimed to be the fall guy of a conspiracy?

Sirhan's lawyers, William F. Pepper and Laurie Dusek claim recordings prove 13 shots were fired on the night Robert Kennedy died while Sirhan's small pistol could only fire eight bullets.

Photograph of Sirhan Sirhan in Custody.
FBI Photo, Public Domain

Robert F. Kennedy.

Public domain FBI Photo.

CHAPTER XXI

POWER

Ronald Reagan in referring to power, once claimed, *"Concentrated power has always been the end of liberty."*

"What Lyndon Johnson wants, above all else, is a return to power. He adores power. And he will endure anything to know that heady sensation again." O'Reilly, p. 144

"Anything." *Ibid.*

Catherine the Great is quoted as saying:

"Power without a nations' confidence is nothing."

A combination of the FBI Chief and the President of the United States as possible co-conspirators for an assassination is a concentration of power that never before existed in our country. The possibility of that combination covering up a Presidential assassination is enormous.

Logic and reason points the inquiring mind in the direction of a top down conspiracy starting with the Vice President.

Biographers before me have documented Lyndon Johnson's corruption, envy, jealousy, dishonesty, hatreds and quest for power.

J. Edgar Hoover must have been really disappointed when the CIA was formed for international espionage and covert activities, while the FBI became limited to domestic crimes. What a challenge to conspire a domestic covert operation must have been for Hoover, to take out a President and cover it up.

Hoover's hatred of Robert Kennedy and Martin Luther King Jr., are well known. His never wanting to give up the directorship of the FBI is also well known.

Hoover and Johnson together realizing they are both out of power if JFK is re-elected are the most logical conspirators for the JFK assassination.

Logical, yes! Reasonable, yes! Who else could cover it up an assassination of an American President, so successfully.

An abuse of power, used to the maximum.

Thomas Jefferson warned us of such abuse by stating:

"I hope our wisdom will grow with our power, and teach us that the less we use our power the greater it will be."

With the published Warren Report ten months after the Assassination, the American public seemed to be satisfied that Oswald did it, as he was presented as some kind of a nut case.

If it is true that the culprits of this conspiracy were Johnson and Hoover, they got away with it, untouched, and free to plan a second assassination.

With most questioning settled by the Warren Report with public acceptance that Oswald did it and was murdered. The next surprise was the assassination of Martin Luther King, Jr., followed five months later by the assassination of Democratic contender for President, Robert F. Kennedy.

Since that time 50 years ago, I have travelled the world and visited more than 100 countries. I talk to the people and yearn to learn their history and customs. The subject of the Kennedy assassination inevitably comes up. Europeans, Asians and South Americans wonder what's the big deal?

'What do you mean", I ask?

It happens, all around the world. Do you think Americans are immune to a change of government by assassination?

I had to admit, we are not immune. We just have trouble acknowledging that it can happen here.

Maybe it is time we used logic and reason instead of believing the conclusions ordered to be printed and distributed by the conspirators themselves.

It is not easy for any of us in a Democracy to even consider there may be evil at the very top of our elected government. We are in a Democracy that is supposed to have checks and balances to prevent such a concentration of power.

Our founding fathers were such brilliant men, who saw the danger placing so much power in the wrong hands.

"Power is not alluring to pure minds." *Thomas Jefferson*

Pure minds are what we desire to elect. Instead, we get power mongers, wolves in sheep's clothing pretending to be skilled leaders, when in fact they are criminals.

If Democracy has a flaw, it is the possibility that evil can rise to the top. President Johnson replaced John F. Kennedy in 1963, upon Kennedy's death as our constitution allows.

"We the people," elected President Johnson in 1964 and he knowing it is against the law, confirmed J. Edgar Hoover as FBI Director for life.

Both, became so powerful that they are above the law, and can do whatever they like.

Their five year plan during the Johnson administration is to rid themselves of both Martin Luther King, Jr. and Robert Kennedy.

The obvious question arises, once Johnson attained the presidency, why should he bother to have the assassination of Martin Luther King Jr., and Robert Kennedy?

Because a deal is a deal. Hoover promised Johnson the presidency with a successful Kennedy assassination. Johnson promised Hoover lifetime directorship of the FBI that would not be possible if Robert Kennedy is elected President.

Martin Luther King Jr. was also getting too powerful in influencing the African-American vote and his massive peaceful civil-disobedience demonstrations were becoming a problem for both Johnson and Hoover.

Using the proven principles of the JFK assassination, where a very confused person is chosen to take the blame, the assassinations were so much easier the second time and the third time.

Photograph of President, Lyndon B. Johnson.
Public Domain, White House Photograph

CHAPTER XXII

COMPARING THE ASSASSINS

If we compare the three Assassins we can see a common thread.

All three assassins are losers.

All three lack a defined purpose in life.

All three are unhappy.

All three are explainable to the American public as irrational.

All three are expendable as scapegoats in a conspiracy.

> Oswald, a Communist, with Soviet experience.

> Ray, a segregationist, in an era of integration.

> Sirhan, a Palestinian, with a hatred of Israel.

All three are carefully chosen by conspirators to assassinate those in power.

Time frame:

All three assassinations occurred with a 5 year period 1963-1968.

Resulting in?

Lyndon B. Johnson, becoming President of the United States, and J. Edgar Hoover gaining the FBI Directorship for life.

The Warren report concludes that there was no conspiracy.

What do you think?

Why did Robert Kennedy sign off, as agreeing with the Warren Report conclusion of no conspiracy?

Because the report was concerned about a conspiracy between Oswald and Ruby or a conspiracy organized by the Soviets or Cuba. The Warren Report made that point clear. RFK understood that the Soviets and Cuba and Oswald and Ruby were not the planners of a conspiracy.

Nowhere in the Warren Report was there an investigation of the two power hungry conspirators who had the most to gain.

Why?

The Report was ordered by the President of the United States and you don't mess with the FBI.

That's why!

The report's conclusions are the same conclusions as the FBI Chief, J. Edgar Hoover's conclusions, ten months earlier.

"Oswald acted alone."

"There was no conspiracy."

Is anyone surprised?

APOTHEOSIS!

"Our Assassinated Leaders, the three most mourned Americans since FDR, hauntingly watch over Arlington National Cemetery.

For Esquire's definitive 35th Anniversary issue, in a hagiographic fantasy, we pay homage to an Idealized, saint-like John Kennedy,

Robert Kennedy and Dr. Martin Luther King in this dreamlike epitaph on the murder of American goodness."

George Lois

Artwork. Courtesy of George Lois

CHAPTER XXIII

LOGIC AND REASON

Using Logic and Reason one asks the question:

Who had the most to gain from the assassination of President Kennedy?

Vice President Lyndon Johnson.

Could he do it alone?

No!

Could he cover it up?

No.

Who else stands to benefit from an assassination of President Kennedy?

FBI Chief, J. Edgar Hoover faces mandatory retirement at age 70.

Can Hoover provide the necessary cover up?

Yes.

What can the Vice President Johnson promise Hoover?

Career Longevity, no forced retirement AND no replacement by Bobby Kennedy whom they both despise.

What about Bobby Kennedy?

He will be their third assassination of the conspiracy.

With the FBI involved, do the assassinations have possibilities of success?

Yes.

Who proposed this conspiracy?

Either Vice President Johnson or FBI Chief Hoover as they both had so much to gain. They have been friends since Johnson was a Congressman when they were neighbors in Washington, D.C.

The FBI has access to social outcasts and misfits in Texas and across the United States, capable of sniper activity.

Lee Harvey Oswald fit's the bill as the sniper or sniper patsy.

FBI lines up additional snipers in the event Oswald misses.

Jack Ruby, fit's the bill as murderer of Oswald, to prevent him from talking.

Ruby, easily bribed, with promise of fame as the man who killed Kennedy's assassin.

Motorcade route established on November 18th, 1963, to pass by Texas School Book Depository.

By November 19th, the Presidential Motorcade route was printed in the Dallas newspapers.

On November 22nd, 1963, President John F. Kennedy is assassinated and taken to Parkland Hospital where he is pronounced dead.

J. Edgar Hoover calls Attorney General, Robert Kennedy to inform him that his brother, President John F. Kennedy is dead.

Lyndon Banes Johnson calls Attorney General Robert Kennedy for instructions on the swearing-in of the new President.

CHAPTER XXIV

EPILOGUE

The era of an FBI Director serving 48 years is over and hopefully should never be repeated.

A Federal statute enacted in 1976 states:

"A Director may not serve more than one 10 year term."

Those mentioned in this book, suspected through logic and reason of a conspiracy to assassinate President John F. Kennedy, have all passed away during this 50 year period.

The same is true for the logical conspirators of the assassination of Martin Luther King Jr. and Presidential nominee, Robert F. Kennedy.

Only Sihran Sihran, remains still alive in prison and no one believes he is capable of organizing a top down conspiracy.

The cover-up accomplished in these three assassinations were so well done, that the conspirators were never discovered, prosecuted and imprisoned. Instead we are left with the Warren Report that concluded Oswald did it alone and there was no evidence of a conspiracy.

The remaining two assassinations follow the same prescription of finding and employing a "patsy" to take the rap for the assassination.

Now fifty years later, time is running short for someone still alive, that was either involved in, or knew of such a top down conspiracy, to come forward and shed light on this subject.

If that were to happen, those who depend on their use of logic and reason could finally conclude that the conspirators have been identified.

Perhaps someone involved knows why Oswald's short statement to the press was, "I'm just a patsy."

APPENDIX I

ATTEMPTS TO ASSASSINATE PRESIDENTS SINCE 1963

1963	John F. Kennedy	Successful

Lee Harvey Oswald is blamed and murdered by Jack Ruby who later dies of cancer.

1968	Robert Kennedy	Successful

A Presidential Candidate for the Democratic Party in 1968 intending to challenge incumbent President Lyndon Johnson was US Senator Robert F. Kennedy a younger brother of John F. Kennedy. He was assassinated on June 5th, 1968 by Sirhan Sirhan with four bullets.

1974	Richard Nixon	Unsuccessful

Samuel Byck attempted hijack plane to crash into White House, suicide.

1975	Gerald Ford	Unsuccessful

Two attempts, Leonette Fromme and Sara Jane Moore, both Life in Prison.

1981	Ronald Reagan	Unsuccessful

John Hinkley Jr. found insane and institutionalized.

1996	Bill Clinton	Unsuccessful
	Osama bin Laden was behind a plot to bomb motorcade.	
2001	George W. Bush	Unsuccessful
	Robert Pickett shot at the White House and served 3 years in prison.	
2011	Barack Obama	Unsuccessful
	Oscar Ramiro Ortega-Hernandez charged with attempted assassination.	

Source. Los Angeles Times Data Desk, 2013.

BIBLIOGRAPHY

Aronson. Marc, *Master of Deceit, J. Edgar Hoover and America in the Age of Lies,* 2012. Candlelwick Press, Somerville, MA.

Brown, Walt, *Treachery In Dallas,* 1995. Carroll & Graf Publishers, Inc. New York, NY.

Califano, Joseph A., Jr., *The Triumph and Tragedy of Lyndon Johnson*, The White House Years, 1991. Simon 7Schuster, New York, NY.

Caro, Robert A, *The Passage of Power, The Years of Lyndon Johnson,* 2012. Alfred A. Knoff, a Division of Random House, New York, NY.

Cross, Robin, *JFK, A Hidden Life.* 1992, C.E. Tuttle Boston, MA.

Dallek, Robert, *Portrait of a President, Lyndon B. Johnson*, 2004. (p. 575.) Oxford University Press, New York, NY.

Davie, Michael, *LBJ, A Foreign Observer's Viewpoint*, 1966. Duell, Sloan and Pierce, New York.

Douglass, James W., JFK and the Unspeakable, Why He died and Why it Matters, 2009. Orbis Books, Maryknoll, New York.

Gentry, Curt, *J. Edgar Hoover, The Man and His Secrets*, 1991. W.W. Norton Company, New York, NY.

Gillon, Steven M, *The Kennedy Assassination—24 Hours After, Lyndon B. Johnson's Pivotal First Day as President,* 2009. Basic Books, A member of Perseus Books Group, New York.

Hilty, James W., *Robert Kennedy, Brother, Protector*, 1997. Temple Univresity Press, Philadelphia, PA.

Holland, Max, *The Kennedy Assassination Tapes, The White House conversations of Lyndon B. Johnson regarding the assassination, the Warren Commission and the aftermath,* 2004. Alfred A. Knoff, New York p.231, 289 relate to President.

Johnson's conversations with Jacqueline Kennedy.

Kantor, Seth, *Who Was Jack Ruby*, 1978. Everest House Publishers, New York, NY.

La Fontaine, Ray and Mary, *Oswald Talked, The New Evidence in the JFK Assassination*, 1996. Pelican Publishing Company, Gretna, Louisiana.

Lifton, David S. *Best Evidence, Disguise and Deception in the Assassination of John F. Kennedy*, 1980. Mcmillan Publishing Co. Inc., New York, NY.

Livingston, Harrisin Edward, *Killing the Truth, Deceit and Deception in the JFK Case,* 1993. Carroll & Graf Publishers, Inc., New York, NY.

Los Angeles Times Data Desk, 2013. *Assassinations. Los* Angeles, *CA.*

Manchester, William, *The Death of A President*, 1967. Harper & Row, New York, NY.

Matthews, Chris, *Jack Kennedy, Elusive Hero*, 2011. Simon & Schuster, New York, NY.

McClellan, Barr, *Blood, Money and Power,* 2003. Hannover House, New York, NY.

McKnight, Gerald D., *The Last Crusade, Martin Luther King Jr., and the Poor Peoples Campaign,* 1998. Westview Press, A Division of Harper Collins, Publishers, Inc., Boulder, CO.

Melanson, Philip, *The Robert Kennedy Assassination, New Revelations on the Conspiracy and Cover-up, 1968-1991,* 1991. Shapolsky Publishers, Inc., New York.

Messich, Hank, *John Edgar Hoover, A critical examination of the Director* McKay Company, Inc., New York.

Moldea, Dan E., *The Killing of Robert Kennedy,* An Investigation of Motive, Means and Opportunity, 1995. W.W. Norton & Co., New York, NY.

Morrow, Robert D, *The Senator Must Die, The Murder of Robert F. Kennedy,* 1988. Roundtable Publishing, Santa Monica, CA

Newman, John, *Oswald and the CIA,* 1995. Carroll & Graf Publishers, Inc., New York, NY.

North, Mark, *Act of Treason. The Role of J. Edgar Hoover in the Assassination of President Kennedy,* 1991. Carroll & Graff Publishers Inc., New York, NY.

O'Riley, Bill and Dugant, Martin, *Killing Kennedy, The End of Camelot,* 2013. Henry Holt and Company, LLC, New York, New York.

O'Sullivan, Shane. *Who Killed Bobby?* The Unsolved Murder of Robert F. Kennedy, 2008. Union Square Press, New York, NY.

O'Toole, George, *The Assassination Tapes. An Electronic Probe into the Murder of John F. Kennedy,* 1975. Penthouse Press, Ltd., New York.

Pepper, William, *An Act of State, The Execution of Martin Luther King,* 2003, Verso Books, New York, NY.

Peters, Charles, *Lyndon B. Johnson, The American Presidents Series*, 2010. Times Books, Henry Holt & Company, New York.

Posner, Gerald, *Case Closed, Lee Harvey Oswald and the Assassination of JFK*, 1993, Random House, New York.

Powers, Richard Gid, *Secrecy and Power, The Life of J. Edgar Hoover*, 1987. The Free Press, Collier Macmillan Publishers, New York, NY.

Schlesinger, *A Thousand Days,* Special Counsel to the Late President. 1965, Harper & Row, Publishers, New York, NY.

Sorensen, Theodore C., *The Kennedy I Knew, Part Two,* 1965. Look Magazine, August 2, 1965.

Streissguth, Tom, *J. Edgar Hoover, Powerful FBI Director,* 2002. Enslow Publishers, Berkley Heights, NJ.

Sullivan, Shane, *Who Killed Bobby? The Unsolved Murder of Robert F. Kennedy*, 2008. Union Square Press, An Imprint of Sterling Publishing Co.,Inc., New York.

Updegrove, Mark K., *Indomitable Will, LBJ in the Presidency*, 2012. Crown Publishers, A Division of Random House, Inc., New York, NY.

Warren, Earl, Chief Justice, 1964. *The President's Commission on the Assassination of President John F. Kennedy.* U.S. Government Printing Office.

White, Theodore, *The Making of the President* 1961. Athenaeum, New York.

Wills, Garry and Demaris, Ovid, *Jack Ruby,* 1967. The New American Library, Inc., New York, NY.

Wikipedia, Useful data provided on Sirhan Sirhan and James Earl Ray, 2013.

ACKNOWLEDGEMENTS

During the process of writing this book, I am thankful to the following for their advice and encouragement to publish.

Duncan Edwards
William Henry Herries
Audrey Marsh
Elizabeth Mathews
Olivia-Irene Rockman
Sherri Lee and John Wilfong
Joe Vasquez

And for so many mentors along the way.

Alberta and John P. Roach
Jim Ibey, Franchi Construction Co.
Henry Moritz, ITT, Federal Electric Co.
General Saleen, ITT, Federal Electric Co.
Al Cushing, System Development Corporation
Joe Kuhn, IBM
William Holbrook, Contractor
Joe King, IBM
Dr. Jack Baxter, MD
Henry J. Maloney, CLU, MONY
Dr. Jozsef Popp, PhD, D.Sc

ABOUT THE AUTHOR

John P. Roach Jr.

Brought up in Glen Rock, NJ, and attained a Liberal Arts Education through study of the Classics, Philosophy and Political Science at St. Michael's College in Vermont. He went on to take additional study on campus in his fields of interest at Seton Hall University, USC University of Southern California, Notre Dame University and Farleigh Dickinson University for Psychology, University of Vermont for Music and most recently Screenwriting at UCLA.

Currently residing in San Diego, CA., he has traveled the world and has completed many screenplays and books on such diverse subjects as classical music, psychology, history, archeology, philosophy, opera, science, bigotry, world travel, politics, love and war.